Default Estimation for Low-Default Portfolios

Nicholas M. Kiefer_
Departments of Economics and Statistical Sciences,
Cornell University,
490 Uris Hall, Ithaca, NY 14853-7601, US.
email:nmk1@cornell.edu
US Department of the Treasury
Office of the Comptroller of the Currency
Risk Analysis Division, 250 E. St. SW, DC 20219

OCC Economics Working Paper 2006-2

August, 2006

Abstract

The problem in default probability estimation for low-default portfolios
is that there is little relevant historical data information. No amount of
data processing can fix this problem. More information is required.
Incorporating expert opinion formally is an attractive option.
Keywords: Bayesian inference, Bayesian estimation, expert
information, Basel II, risk management
JEL Classi.cations: C11, C13, C44, G18, G32

1 Introduction

The Basel II framework (Basel Committee on Banking Supervision (2004)) for
capital standards provides for (some) banks to use models to assess risks and

_Disclaimer: The statements made and views expressed herein are solely those of the author,
and do not represent official policies, statements or views of the Office of the Comptroller of the
Currency or its staff. Acknowledgement: I thank Jeffrey Brown, Mike Carhill, Hwansik Choi,
Erik Larson, Mark Levonian, Anirban Mukherjee, Mitch Stengel, and seminar participants at
Cornell University and the OCC. These thanks come with gratitude but without any implication
of agreement with my views.

determine minimum capital requirements. All aspects of the models – specification, estimation, validation – will have to meet the scrutiny of national supervisors. The presumption is that these models will be the same ones that sophisticated institutions use to manage their loan portfolios. Banks using internal ratings-based (IRB) methods to calculate credit risks must calculate default probabilities (PD), loss given default (LGD), exposure at default (EAD) and effective maturity (M) for groups of homogeneous assets. For very safe assets, calculations based on historical data may "not be sufficiently reliable" Basel Committee on Banking Supervision (2005) to form a probability of default estimate, since so few defaults are observed. This issue has attracted attention in the literature, for example Balthazar (2004), and methods which advocate departing from the usual unbiased estimator have been proposed by Pluto and Tasche (2005). In this paper I argue that uncertainty about the default probability should be modeled the same way as uncertainty about defaults – namely, represented in a probability distribution. A future default either occurs or doesn't (given the definition). Since we do not know whether it occurs or not, we model this uncertain event with a probability distribution. This model reflects our partial knowledge of the default mechanism. Similarly, the default probability is unknown. But experts do know something about the latter, and we can represent this knowledge in a probability distribution. Inference should be based on a probability distribution for the default probability. The final distribution should reflect both data and expert information. This combining of information is easy to do, using Bayes rule, given that information is represented in probability distribution. The result is an estimator which is different from the unbiased estimator, but which moves the unbiased estimator toward an expert opinion rather than simply bounding it away from zero.

For convenience and ease of exposition I focus here on estimating the default probability θ for a portfolio of safe assets. Section 2 treats the specification of the likelihood function and indicates what might be expected from the likelihood function. General comments on the modeling of uncertainty through probabilities, the standard approach to default modeling, are made in Section 3. Section 4 considers the role of expert information about the unknown default probability and how that might be represented. Specifically, it is represented in a probability distribution, for exactly the same reasons that uncertainty about defaults is represented in a probability distribution. Combination of expert and data information is taken up in Section 5, following, for example, DeGroot (1970). Section 6 considers elicitation of an expert's information and its representation in a probability distribution. Section 7 treats the inferences that could be made on the basis of the expert information and likely data information. Although no data are at hand, it is possible in the low-default case to consider all likely data realizations in particular samples. Section 8 compares the information in the expert information with the information in the data. The data information will dominate for large sample sizes, the usual result, but large here is hopelessly unrealistic. Section 9 considers additional inference issues and supervisory issues. Section 10 concludes.

2   The likelihood function

Expert judgement is crucial at every step of a statistical analysis. To emphasize this fact, I will use the notation e to indicate information provided by expert judgement. It is not really necessary to distinguish objective from subjective judgement at this stage. That is, the expert knowledge could be the result of accumulated experience with similar problems and data, or simply the result of knowledgeable consideration. Typical data consist of a number of asset/years for a group of similar assets. In each year, there is either a default or not. This is a clear simplification of the actual problem, in which asset quality can improve or deteriorate and assets are not completely homogeneous. Nevertheless, it is useful to model the problem as one of independent Bernoulli sampling with unknown parameter θ. Let d_i indicate whether the ith observation was a default ($d_i = 1$) or not ($d_i = 0$). A convenient and widely chosen (as a result of judgement) model for the distribution of d_i is $p(d_i|\theta, e) = \theta^{d_i}(1 - \theta)^{1-d_i}$. Let $D = \{d_i, i = 1, ..., n\}$ denote the whole data set and $r = r(D) = \sum_i d_i$ the count of defaults. Then the joint distribution of the data is

$$
\begin{aligned}
p(D|\theta, e) &= \prod \theta^{d_i}(1 - \theta)^{1-d_i} \qquad (2.1)\\
&= \theta^r(1 - \theta)^{n-r}
\end{aligned}
$$

As a function of θ for given data D, this is the likelihood function $L(\theta|D, e)$. Since this distribution depends on the data D only through r (n is regarded as fixed), the sufficiency principle implies that we can concentrate attention on the

3

distribution of r

$$p(r|\theta, e) = \binom{n}{r}\theta^r(1 - \theta)^{n-r} \tag{2.2}$$

The role of expert judgement is not usually explicitly indicated at this stage, so it is worthwhile to point to its contribution. First, what should be the statistical model? The independent Bernoulli model is not the only possibility. Certainly independence is a strong assumption and would have to be considered carefully. Note that independence here is conditional independence. The marginal (with respect to θ; see below) distribution of D certainly exhibits dependence. It is through this dependence that the data are informative on the default probability. Second, are the observations identically distributed? Perhaps the default probabilities differ across assets, and the most risky generally default first. Third, what exactly constitutes a default? Fourth, what assets can reasonably be modelled as belonging to the homogeneous group? Risk modelers are acutely aware of these issues and modelers can expect to have to justify their specifications to validators. The whole process is subject to supervisory review. See OCC (2006).

Regarded as a function of θ for given data, 2.2 is the likelihood function $L(\theta|r, e)$. Since $r(D)$ is a sufficient statistic, no other function of the data is informative about θ given $r(D)$. All of the relevant data information on θ comes through the distribution $p(r|\theta, e)$. Formally, the observed information (the negative second derivative of the logarithm of the joint data density with respect to the parameter) is

$$
\begin{aligned}
-d^2 \ln p(D|\theta, e)/d\theta^2 &= -d^2 \ln p(r|\theta, e)/d\theta^2 \tag{2.3}\\
&= (r/\theta^2 + (n - r)/(1 - \theta)^2). \tag{2.4}
\end{aligned}
$$

The strict implication is that no amount of data-massaging or data-processing can improve the data evidence on θ. Figures 1 and 2 graph the normed likelihood functions $\overline{L}(\theta|r, e) = L(\theta|r, e)/\max_\theta L(\theta|r, e)$ for $r = 0, 1, 2, 5$, and $n =100$ and 500. These figures illustrate the sorts of observed likelihood functions one might see in practice.

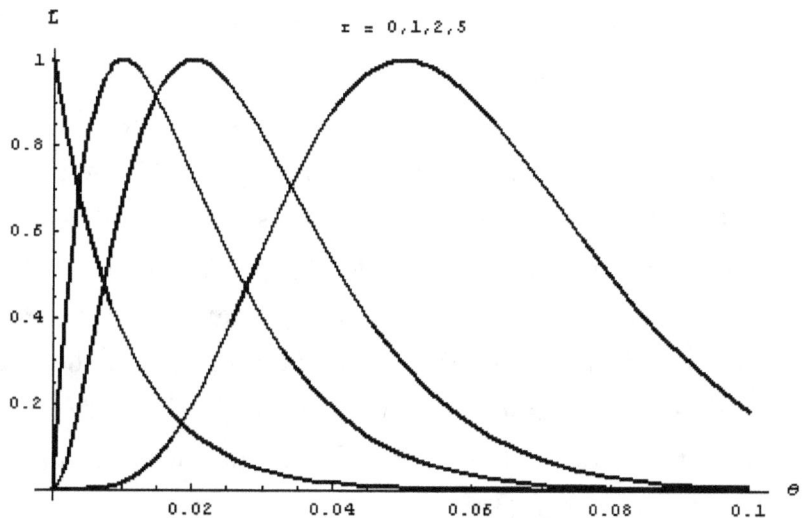

Figure 1: Likelihood Functions, n=100. Functions move to the right with
increasing r.

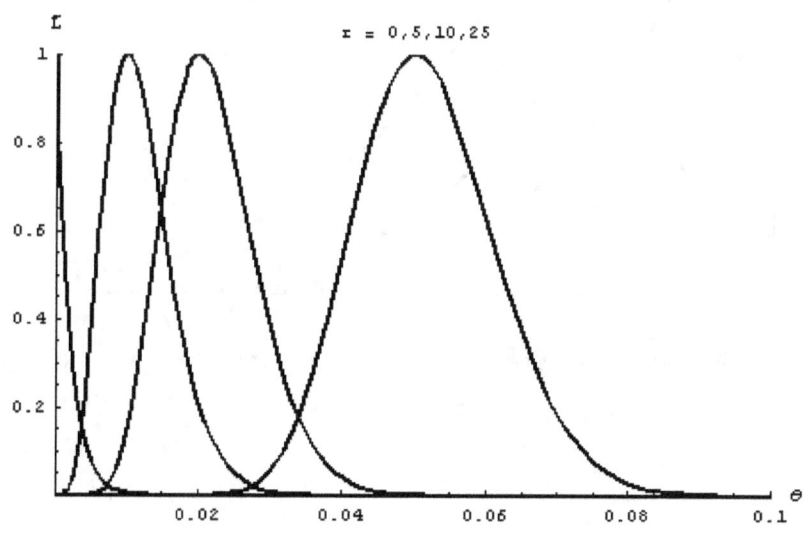

Figure 2: Likelihood Functions, n=500. Functions move to the right with
increasing r.

Figures 1 and 2 illustrate that small changes in the realized number of defaults
can have a substantial effect on the maximum likelihood estimator (MLE). Thus,
for n=100, an increase by 1 in the number of defaults increases the MLE by .01.
If the probability being estimated is large (e.g., 0.3), then a difference in the
estimate of 0.01 is not, perhaps, as dramatic as when the realistic values are 0.01

or 0.02. Further, these small estimates are sharply determined, according to the shape of the likelihood functions.

A different point of view can be illustrated by the expected likelihood function for a given hypothetical value of θ. Figures 3 and 4 plot $\sum_j \overline{L}(\theta|r_j, e)p(r_j|\theta_0, e)$ for $\theta_0 =0.005$, 0.01, 0.02, and 0.05 and $n=100,500$. This function is rather more spread than the likelihood on given data (note that $\overline{L}(\theta|r, e)$ is concave in r for values near the most likely value $n\theta$). Perhaps these figures are better than the previous for considering what the data might be able to tell us, though that is still problematic since these are plots for given hypothetical values of θ. A better plot for considering what the data might say would take into account not only that r is uncertain but also that θ is uncertain.

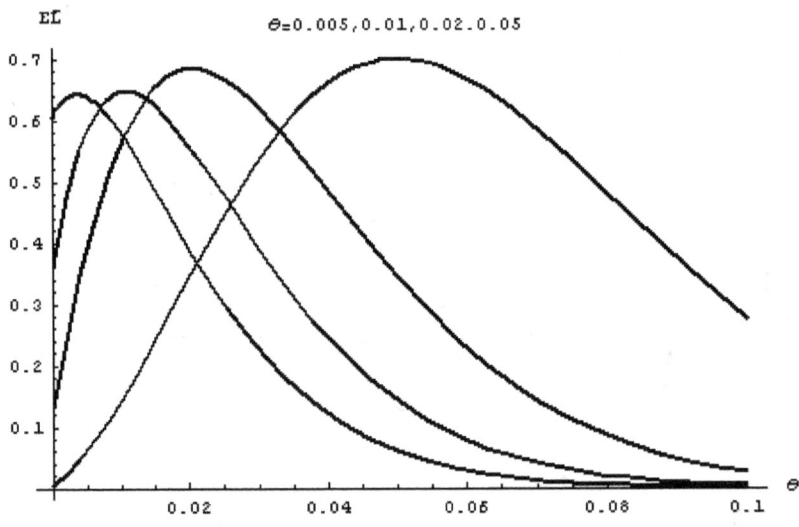

Figure 3: Expected Likelihood, n=100. Functions move to the right with increasing θ_0.

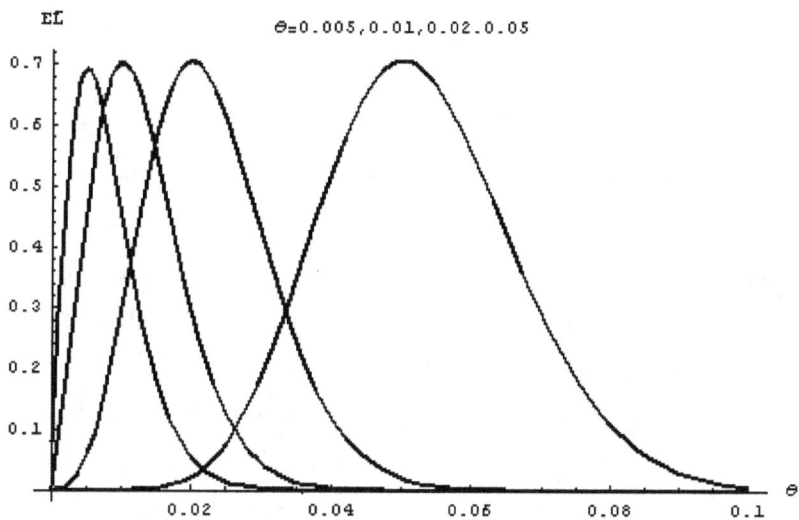

Figure 4: Expected Likelihood, n=500. Functions move to the right with increasing θ_0.

3   Uncertainty and probability

The statistical model above is a framework for organizing and quantifying uncertainty about defaults. That is, in a group of n asset/years, we can identify particular events, such as A ="observation 1, and only observation 1, defaults," B = "observation 2, and only observation 2, defaults," C = "observation 1 defaults," D ="observation 2 defaults," etc. These events are uncertain events and we need a system by which to measure the uncertainty and to combine the uncertainties consistently. It is standard in the application to defaults to use a probabilistic model. We choose a standard by which to measure the uncertainty; for example we might reason that the chance that observation one defaults is about the same as the chance of drawing a red ball at random from an urn containing $n\theta$ red balls and n total red and black balls. The associated probabilities given a value of θ are $P(A|\theta, e) = \theta(1 - \theta)^{n-1}$, $P(B|\theta, e) = \theta(1 - \theta)^{n-1}$, $P(C|\theta, e) = \theta$, and $P(D|\theta, e) = \theta$. The probabilities are useful for thinking about uncertainty because of the way they combine. Aggregating uncertainties by combining probabilities is the key to moving from uncertainty about whether an asset will default, to default rates in a segment of homogeneous assets, to defaults in the whole diversified portfolio, and to the probability that the bank itself will default. Thus the probability that one or the other of the mutually exclusive events A and B occurs is $P(A\ or\ B|\theta, e) = P(A|\theta, e) + P(B|\theta, e)$. This formula is the key to the $\binom{n}{r}$ factor

7

in $p(r|\theta, e)$; we are summing over all the ways r defaults can occur in n observations. It is called the *addition rule* for probabilities. The probability that two events occur is $P(C \text{ and } D|\theta, e) = P(C|D, \theta, e)P(D|\theta, e)$. This formula holds whether or not C and D are independent. It is the *multiplication rule*. These two rules, together with a third, *convexity*; which is $0 \leq P(A|B, \theta, e) \leq 1$ and $P(A|A, \theta, e) = 1$, are sometimes stated as axioms underlying a system of probabilities. It seems compelling that beliefs about uncertain events, here configurations of defaults, should combine in accordance with these axioms, and hence the proper description of uncertainty is through probabilities. This description comes to hand naturally when we model physical phenomena. Indeed, this method of describing uncertainty is enforced by the choice of a probability model for defaults.

There is much literature on this topic. See Jaynes (2003) and for a classic reference Lindley (1953). The next logical step is to extend the reasoning about uncertain defaults to reasoning about uncertain default probabilities.

4 Expert opinion

It is absolutely clear that there is some information available about θ in addition to the data information. For example, we expect that the portfolio in question is a low-default portfolio. Where does this expectation come from? We would be surprised if θ for such a portfolio turned out to be, say, 0.2. Further, there is a presumption that no portfolio has default probability 0. Can this information be organized and incorporated in the analysis in a sensible way? Yes. This involves quantification of the information or, alternatively, quantification of the uncertainty about θ.

Quantification of uncertainty requires comparison with a standard, just as quantification of a physical property such as length or weight involves comparison with a standard such as a meter or a kilogram. One standard for measuring uncertainty is comparison with a simple experiment, such as drawing balls from an urn at random as above, or sequences of coin flips. We might begin by defining events for consideration. Examples of events are $A = "\theta \leq 0.005"$; $"B = "\theta \leq 0.01"; C = "\theta \leq 0.015,"$ etc. Assign probabilities by comparison; for example, A is about as likely as seeing three heads in 50 throws of a fair coin. Sometimes it is easier to assign probabilities by considering the relative likelihoods of events and their complements. Thus, either A or "*not A*" must occur. Suppose A is considered twice as likely as "*not A*." Then the probability of A is 2/3, since we have fixed the ratio and the probabilities must add up to one. Some prefer to recast this assessment in terms of betting. Thus, the payout x is received if A occurs, (1-x) if not. Again, the events are exhaustive and mutually exclusive. Adjust x until you are indifferent between betting on A and "*not A*." Then, it is reasonable to assume for small bets that $xP(A) = (1-x)(1-P(A))$ or $P(A) = (1-x)$. These possibilities and others are discussed in Berger (1980). It is clear that assessing probabilities requires some thought and some practice, but also that it can be done. It can be shown that beliefs that satisfy certain consistency requirements, for example that the believer is unwilling to make sure-loss bets, lead to measures of uncertainty that combine according to the laws of probability: convexity, additivity and multiplication. See for example DeGroot (1970).[1]

The essence of the discussion is that there is only one satisfactory way of representing uncertainty about θ, just as there is one compelling way to model uncertainty about defaults – namely, through a probability distribution, $p(\theta|e)$. As a practical matter, it is unlikely that $p(\theta|e)$, especially if a parametric form is chosen, will be an exact and accurate description of beliefs. Indeed, it is not clear that beliefs can be assessed in this level of detail, i.e., for each of the infinite set of possible events. This should not dissuade us from pursuing the analysis, however. After all, essentially the same set of objections can be raised at the level of the likelihood – is it an accurate description of the data-generating process, given θ? Are the events truly independent? Are the observations truly trials of the same experiment? No, but we use judgement to conclude that our statistical model captures the essential features of the problem, and that the remaining inaccuracies are minor. There is often, in scientific research, vigorous argument about the validity of the model, but there is also widespread use of statistical models that are obviously wrong but still accurate enough to be useful. The same care should be used in the assessment of the distribution $p(\theta|e)$. Features that really matter should be assessed more carefully than features that do not. As in application of

---

[1]There is a technical issue that arises in reasoning about θ that did not arise in reasoning about the defaults, and that is due to the continuity of θ. Essentially, there are an infinity of possible events and an assumption is needed to avoid paradoxes of infinity. The necessary assumption is some variation of the sure thing principle: if $\{D_k\}$ is a set of mutually exclusive subsets of B, and $\bigcup_k D_k = B$ and if $P(A|D_k) = p$, for all k, then $P(A|B) = p$.

the likelihood, judgement is required.

We next turn away from theory to the practical matter of specifying a functional form for the prior distribution $p(\theta|e)$. The conditioning argument e will be temporarily dropped as we consider properties of potential functional forms for representing uncertainty. A particularly easy specification is the uniform $p(\theta) = 1$ for $\theta \in [0, 1]$. This prior would sometimes be regarded as "uninformative," (with the implied additional property "unobjectionable") since it assigns equal probability to equal length subsets of [0,1]. The mean of this distribution is 1/2; other moments also exist, and in that sense it is indeed informative (a prior expectation of default probability 1/2 might easily not be considered suitable for low-default portfolios). A distribution in common use for a parameter that is constrained to lie in [0,1] is the beta distribution. The beta distribution for the random variable $\theta \in [0, 1]$ with parameters (α, β) is

$$p(\theta|\alpha, \beta) = \frac{\Gamma(\alpha + \beta)}{\Gamma(\alpha)\Gamma(\beta)}\theta^{\alpha-1}(1 - \theta)^{\beta-1} \tag{4.1}$$

A couple of examples of this distribution are graphed in figure 5 ($\{\alpha, \beta\} = \{2, 50\}$ and $\{3.2\}$, along with the uniform distribution.$\{\alpha, \beta\} = \{1, 1\}$).

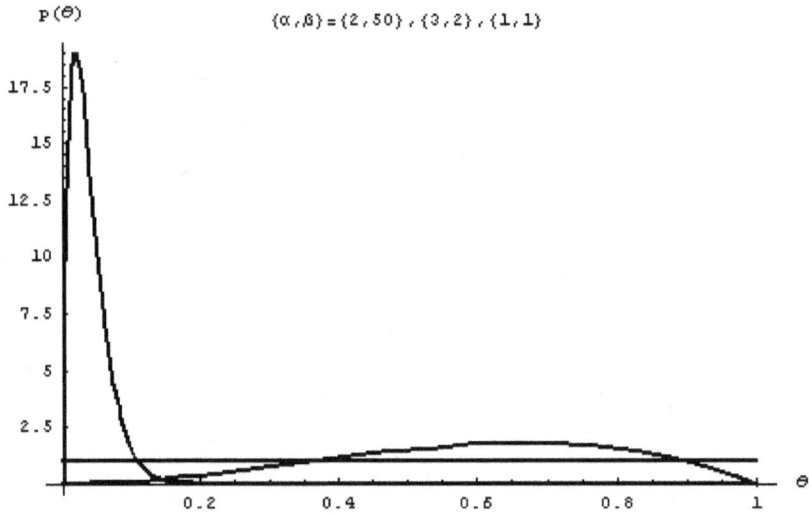

Figure 5: Examples of two-parameter Beta Distributions. The highest has $\{\alpha, \beta\} = \{2, 50\}$, the uniform is $\{1, 1\}$.

The first specification, which has essentially all of its mass below 0.15, a mean of 0.038, and a mode at 0.021, might have the shape most suitable as a prior for the default probability on a low-default portfolio. At present, the purpose here is simply to indicate the sorts of distributions available in this parametric family. A particularly easy generalization is to specify the support $\theta \in [a, b] \subset [0, 1]$. It is possible that some applications would require the support of θ. to consist of the union of disjoint subsets of $[0, 1]$, but this seems fanciful in the current application. A simple starting point is the uniform $p(\theta|e) = 1/(b - a)$. This prior would again sometimes be regarded as "uninformative," since it assigns equal probability to equal length subsets of $[a, b]$. The mean of this distribution is $(a + b)/2$. We may think that this specification is too restrictive, in that consideration might require that intervals near the most likely value should be more probable than intervals near the endpoints. A somewhat richer specification is the beta distribution 4.1 modified to have support $[a, b]$. Let t have the beta distribution and upon change variables to $\theta(t) = a + (b - a)t$ with inverse function $t(\theta) = (\theta - a)/(b - a)$ and Jacobian $dt(\theta)/d\theta = 1/(b - a)$. Then

$$p(\theta|\alpha, \beta, a, b) = \frac{\Gamma(\alpha + \beta)}{(b - a)\Gamma(\alpha)\Gamma(\beta)}((a - \theta)/(a - b))^{\alpha - 1}((\theta - b)/(a - b))^{\beta - 1} \quad (4.2)$$

over the range $\theta \in [a, b]$. This distribution has mean $E\theta = (b\alpha + a\beta)/(\alpha + \beta)$, allowing substantially more flexibility than the uniform. A couple of examples of this distribution on the range [.003,0.2] are graphed in figure 6 (for $\{\alpha, \beta\} = \{2, 5\}$ and $\{3.2\}$, along with the uniform distribution $\{\alpha, \beta\} = \{1, 1\}$).

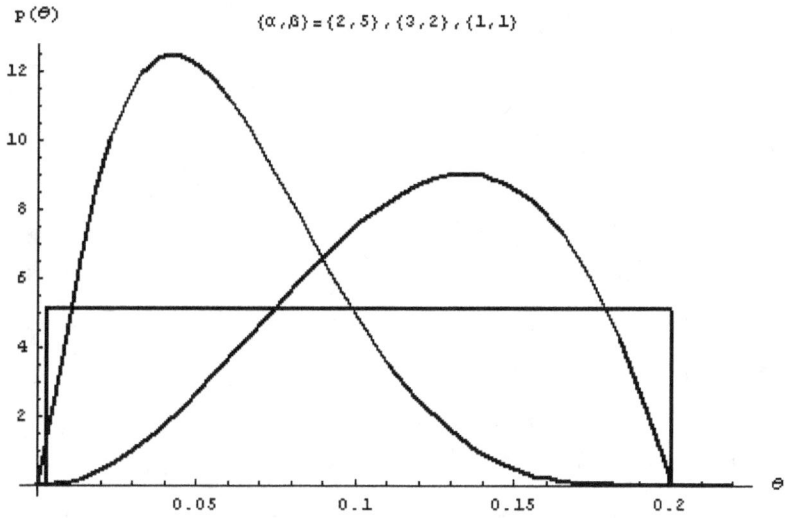

Figure 6: Examples of 4-parameter Beta Distributions. The leftmost peak has $\{\alpha, \beta\} = \{2, 5\}$, the uniform is $\{1, 1\}$.

11

The four-parameter Beta distribution allows flexibility within the range [a,b], but in some situations it may be too restrictive. For example, it is unimodal. This is unlikely to be a problem for representing the prior uncertainty of an individual expert, but it may not be flexible enough to allow combination of information from many experts. A simple generalization is the seven-parameter mixture of two four-parameter Betas with common support. The additional parameters are the two new $\{\alpha, \beta\}$ parameters and the mixing parameter λ.

$$
\begin{aligned}
p(\theta|\alpha_1, \beta_1, \alpha_2, \beta_2, a, b) \quad = \quad & \frac{\lambda \Gamma(\alpha_1 + \beta_1)}{(b-a)\Gamma(\alpha_1)\Gamma(\beta_1)}((a-\theta)/(a-b))^{\alpha_1 - 1}((\theta - b)/(a-b))^{\beta_1 - 1} \\
& + \frac{(1-\lambda)\Gamma(\alpha_2 + \beta_2)}{(b-a)\Gamma(\alpha_2)\Gamma(\beta_2)}((a-\theta)/(a-b))^{\alpha_2 - 1}((\theta - b)/(a-b))^{\beta_2 - 1}
\end{aligned}
$$

Computations with this mixture distribution are not substantially more complicated than computations with the four-parameter Beta alone. If necessary, more mixture components with new parameters can be added, although it seems unlikely that expert information would be detailed and specific enough to require this complicated a representation. There is theory on the approximation of general prior distributions by mixtures of conjugate distributions. By choosing enough Beta-mixture terms the approximation of an arbitrary continuous prior $p(\theta|e)$ for a Bernoulli parameter can be made arbitrarily accurate. See Diaconis and Ylvisaker (1985). Useful references on the choice of prior distribution are Box and Tiao (1992) and Jaynes (2003).

5   Updating (learning)

With $p(\theta|e)$ describing expert opinion and the statistical model for the data information $p(r|\theta, e)$ at hand, we are in a position to combine the expert information with the data information to calculate $p(\theta|r, e)$, the posterior distribution describing the uncertainty about θ after observation of r defaults in n trials. The rules for combining probabilities imply
$P(A|B)P(B) = P(A \text{ and } B) = P(B|A)P(A)$, or more usefully
$P(B|A) = P(A|B)P(B)/P(A)$, assuming $P(A) > 0$. Applying this rule gives

Bayes' rule for updating beliefs

$$p(\theta|r, e) = p(r|\theta, e)p(\theta|e)/p(r|e) \qquad (5.1)$$

The potentially mysterious part of this formula is $p(r|e)$, the unconditional distribution of the number of defaults, which is

$$p(r|e) = \int p(r|\theta, e)p(\theta|e)d\theta. \qquad (5.2)$$

$p(r|e)$ is also called the predictive distribution of the statistic r. For our two-parameter Beta family 4.1, an exact functional form can be calculated. It is

$$p(r|e) = \frac{(\Gamma(r + \alpha)\Gamma(n - r + \beta)\Gamma(\alpha + \beta)\Gamma(n + 1)}{\Gamma(r + 1)\Gamma(n - r + 1)\Gamma(\alpha)\Gamma(\beta)\Gamma(n + \alpha + \beta)} \qquad (5.3)$$

For the special case of the uniform prior with $\alpha = \beta = 1$, this takes the simple form $p(r|e) = 1/(n + 1)$. For the four-parameter Beta family 4.2 and the Beta mixture family, the predictive distributions are not so simple but it are easily calculated. Figure 7 shows the predictive distribution corresponding to the Beta[2,50] prior shown in Figure 5 and for a sample size of 100.

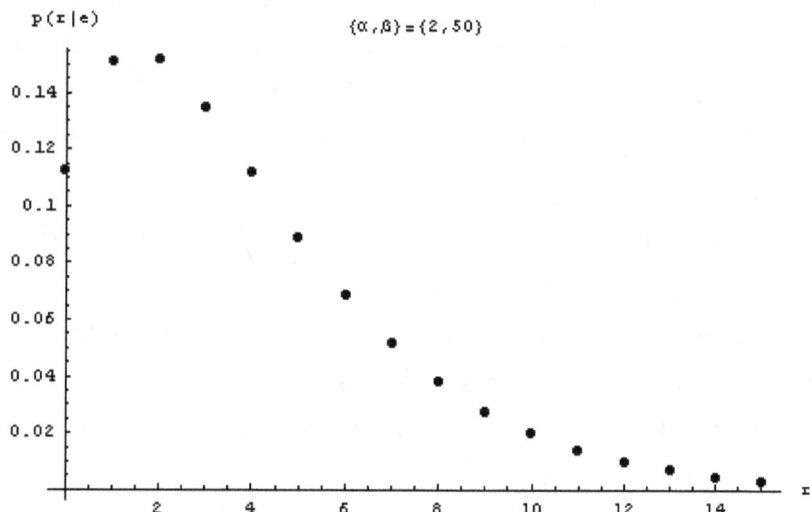

Figure 7: Predictive Distribution p(r|e) for Beta[2,50] Prior

For the purpose of predicting the number of defaults in a portfolio of a given size, the predictive distribution 5.3 is relevant. For inference about the default probability θ, for example for input into the Basel capital formula, the posterior distribution 5.1 is relevant.

Further discussion of the beta-binomial analysis sketched here and of applications to other models is given by Raiffa and Schlaifer (1961). On the Bayesian approach to econometrics see Zellner (1996), a reprint of the influential 1971 edition.

6 Prior Distribution

I have asked an expert to specify a portfolio and give me some aspects of his beliefs about the unknown default probability. The portfolio consists of loans to highly-rated, large, internationally active and complex banks. The method included a specification of the problem and some specific questions over E-mail followed by a discussion. Elicitation of prior distributions is an area that has attracted attention. General discussions of the elicitation of prior distributions are given by Kadane, Dickey, Winkler, Smith, and Peters (1980) and Kadane and Wolfson (1998). An example assessing a prior for a Bernoulli parameter is Chaloner and Duncan (1983). Chaloner and Duncan follow Kadane et al in suggesting that assessments be done not directly on the probabilities concerning the parameters, but on the predictive distribution. That is, questions should be asked about observables, to bring the expert's thoughts closer to familiar ground. Thus, in the case of defaults, a lack of prior knowledge might indicate that the predictive probability of the number of defaults in a sample of size n would be $1/(n+1)$. Departures from this predictive distribution indicate prior knowledge. In the case of a Bernoulli parameter and a two-parameter beta prior, Chaloner and Duncan suggest first eliciting the mode of the predictive distribution for a given n (an integer), then assessing the relative probability of the adjacent values. Graphical feedback is provided for refinement of the specification. Examples consider n=20; perhaps the method would be less attractive for the large sample sizes and low probabilities we anticipate. The suggestion to interrogate experts on what they would expect to see in data, rather than what they would expect of parameter values, is appealing and I have to some extent pursued this with our expert.

It is necessary to specify a period over which to define the default probability. The "true" default probability has probably changed over time. Recent experience may be thought to be more relevant than the distant past, although the sample period should be representative of experience through a cycle. It could be argued that a recent period including the 2001-2002 period of mild downturn covers a modern cycle. A period that included the 1980's would yield higher default probabilities, but these are probably not currently relevant. The default probability of interest is the current and immediate future value, not a guess at what past estimates might be. There are probably 50 or fewer banks in this highly rated category, and a sample period over the last seven years or so might include 300 observations as a high value. We did the elicitation and the calculations to follow assuming a sample of 300 asset/years. For our application, we also considered a "small" sample of 100 observations and a "large" sample of 500 observations, replicating the examples considered above. Considering first the predictive distribution on 300 observations, the modal value was zero defaults. Upon being asked to consider the relative probabilities of zero or one default, conditional on one or fewer defaults occurring, the expert expressed some trepidation as it is difficult to think about such rare events. The expert was quite happy in thinking about probabilities over probabilities, however. This may not be so uncommon in this technical area, as practitioners are accustomed to working with probabilities. The minimum value for the default probability was 0.0001 (one basis point). The expert reported that a value above 0.035 would occur with probability less than 10%, and an absolute upper bound was 0.05. The median value was 0.0033. The expert remarked that the mean at 0.005 was larger than the median. Quartiles were assessed by asking the expert to consider the value at which larger or smaller values would be equiprobable given that the value was less than the median, then given that the value was more than the median. The former seemed easier to think about and was 0.00225 ("between 20 and 25 basis points"). The latter, the .75 quartile, was assessed at .025

This set of answers is more than enough information to determine a four-parameter Beta distribution. I used a method of moments to fit parametric probability statements to the expert assessments. The moments I used were squared differences relative to the target values, for example $((a - 0.0001)/0.0001)^2$. The support points were quite well-determined for a range of $\{\alpha, \beta\}$pairs at the assessed values $\{a, b\} = [0.0001, 0.05]$. These were allowed to vary but the optimization routine did not change them beyond the 7th decimal place. The rather high (?) value of b reflects the long tail apparently desired by the expert. The $\{\alpha, \beta\}$ parameters were rather less well-determined (the sum of squares function was fairly flat) and I settled on the values (1.9, 21.0) as best describing the expert's information. The resulting prior distribution $p(\theta|e)$

is graphed in Figure 8.

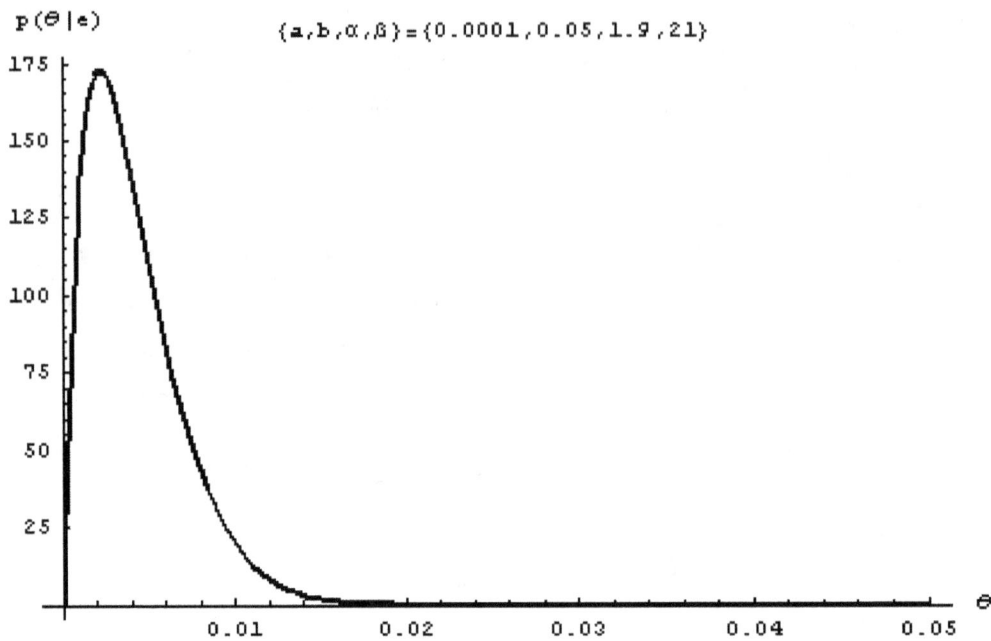

Figure 8: Distribution Reflecting Expert Information

The median of this distribution is 0.0036, the mean is 0.0042. In practice, after the information is aggregated into an estimated probability distribution, then additional properties of the distribution would be calculated and the expert would be consulted again to see if any changes were in order before proceeding to data analysis Lindley (1982). This process would be repeated as necessary. In the present application there was one round of feedback, valuable since the expert had time to consider the probabilities involved. The characteristics reported are from the second round of elicitation. Further rounds were omitted for two reasons. First, we are doing a hypothetical example here, to illustrate the feasibility of all steps of the analysis. Thus the prior should be realistic and should genuinely reflect expert information, but it need not be as painstakingly assessed and refined as in an application. Second, I did not want to annoy the expert beyond the threshold of participation.

The predictive distribution 5.3 corresponding to this prior is given in Figure 9.

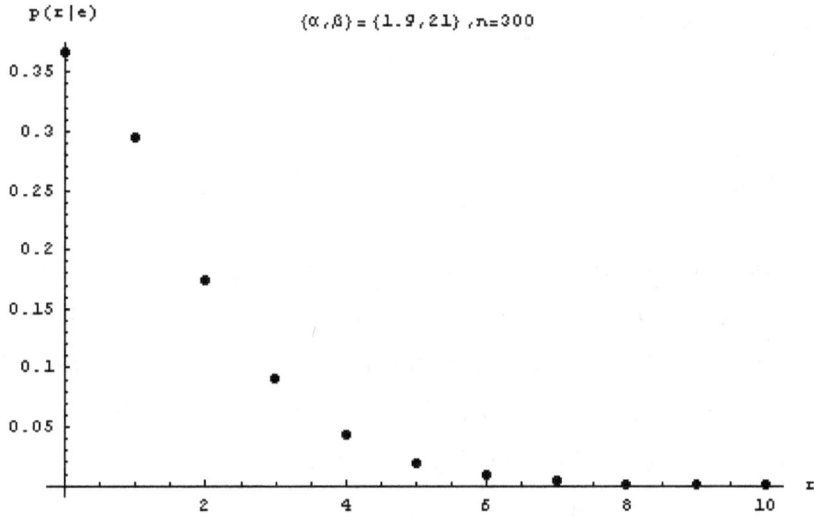

Figure 9: Predictive Distribution $p(r|\theta, e)$

With our specification, the expected value of r, $E(r|e) = \sum\limits_{k=0}^{n} kp(k|e)$ is 0.424 for n=100, 1.27 for n=300 and 2.12 for n=500. Defaults are expected to be rare

events.

It is interesting to compute the unconditional expected likelihood

$$E\overline{L}(\theta|e) = \sum_{j} \overline{L}(\theta|r_j|e)p(r_j|e)$$

for comparison with figures 3 and 4. This is given in figure 10 for n = {100, 300, 500}.

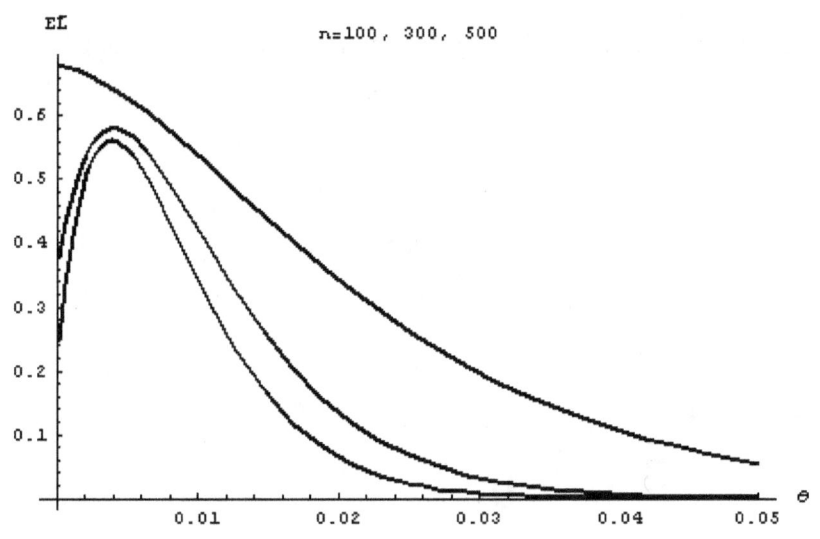

Figure 10: Expected Likelihoods. The highest function is for n=100, the lowest for n=500.

7 Posterior Analysis

The posterior distribution, $p(\theta|r, e)$, is graphed in figure 11 for r = 0, 1, 2 and 5 and n=100; in figure 12 for r = 0, 1, 3 and 10 and n=300, and in figure 13 for r = 0, 2, 10 and 20 and n=500. The corresponding likelihood functions, for comparison, were given in figures 1 and 2. Note the substantial differences in location, even in the n=500, "large-sample" case. Comparison with the prior distribution graphed in Figure 8 reveals that the expert provides much more information to the analysis than do the data.

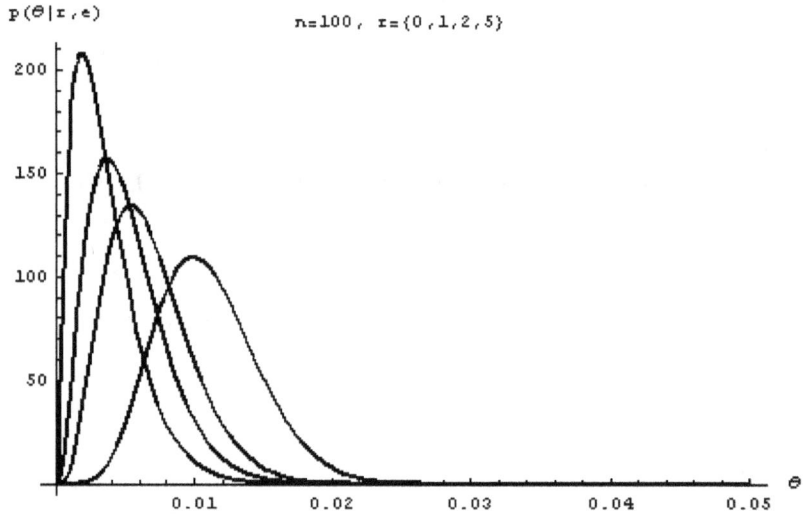

Figure 11: Posterior Distributions $p(\theta|r, e)$ for n=100. Functions move to the right as r increases.

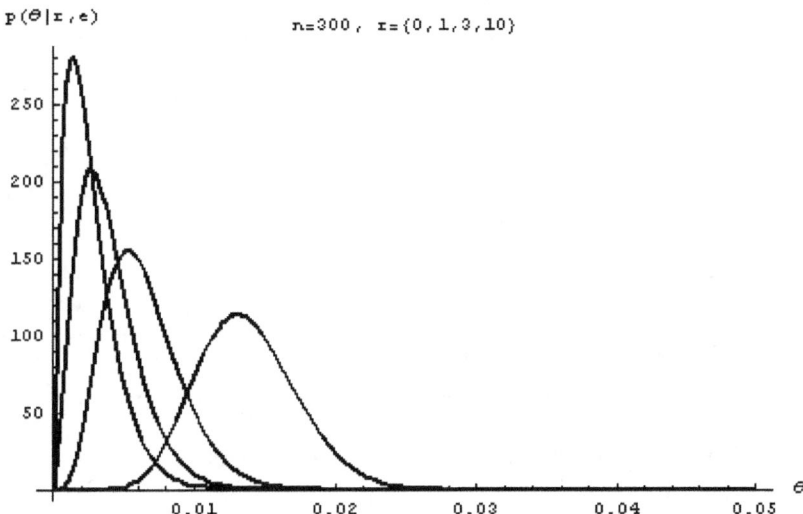

Figure 12: Posterior Distributions $p(\theta|r, e)$ for n=300. Functions move to the right as r increases.

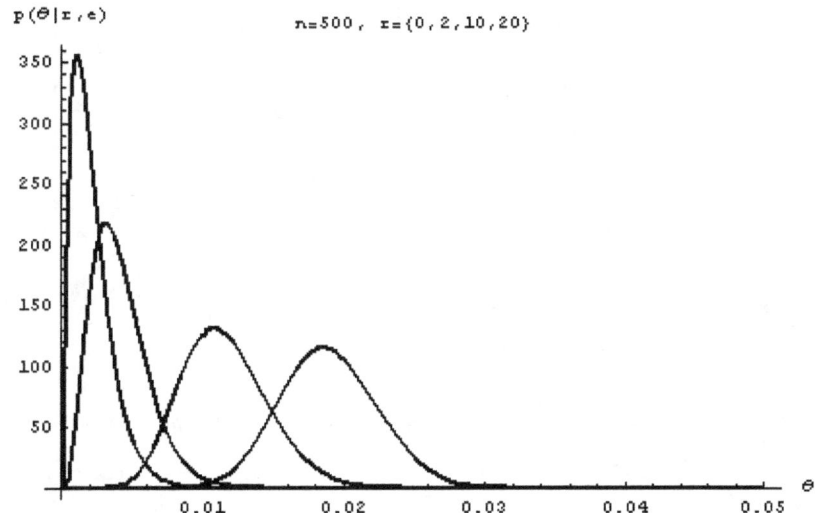

Figure 13: Posterior Distributions $p(\theta|r, e)$ for n=500. Functions move to the right as r increases.

Given the distribution $p(\theta|r, e)$, we might ask for a summary statistic, a suitable estimator for plugging into the required capital formulas as envisioned by the Basel Committee on Banking Supervision (2004). A natural value to use is the posterior expectation, $\overline{\theta} = E(\theta|r, e)$. The expectation is an optimal estimator under quadratic loss and is asymptotically an optimal estimator under a wide variety of loss functions. An alternative, by analogy with the maximum likelihood

19

estimator $\widehat{\theta}$, is the posterior mode $\dot{\theta}$. As a summary measure of our confidence we would use the posterior standard deviation $\sigma_\theta = \sqrt{E(\theta - \overline{\theta})^2}$. By comparison, the usual approximation to the standard deviation of the maximum likelihood estimator is $\sigma_{\widehat{\theta}} = \sqrt{\widehat{\theta}(1 - \widehat{\theta})/n}$. These quantities are given in Table 1 for a variety of combinations of n and r.

n	r	$\overline{\theta}$	$\dot{\theta}$	$\widehat{\theta}$	σ_θ	$\sigma_{\widehat{\theta}}$
100	0	0.0036	0.0018	0.000	0.0024	0 (!).
100	1	0.0052	0.0036	0.010	0.0028	0.0100
100	2	0.0067	0.0053	0.020	0.0031	0.0140
100	5	0.0109	0.0099	0.050	0.0037	0.0218
300	0	0.0027	0.0014	0.000	0.0018	0(!)
300	1	0.0039	0.0027	0.003	0.0022	0.0033
300	3	0.0064	0.0053	0.010	0.0027	0.0057
300	10	0.0137	0.0131	0.033	0.0035	0.0103
500	0	0.0021	0.0011	0.000	0.0015	0 (!)
500	2	0.0041	0.0032	0.004	0.0020	0.0028
500	10	0.0115	0.0108	0.020	0.0031	0.0063
500	20	0.0190	0.0185	0.040	0.0034	0.0088

Table 1: Default Probabilities: Location and Precision

Note: $\overline{\theta}$ is the posterior mean, $\dot{\theta}$ the mode, $\widehat{\theta}$ the MLE, σ_θ the posterior s.d. and $\sigma_{\widehat{\theta}}$ the s.d. of the MLE

Which procedure gives the most useful results for the hypothetical datasets? The maximum-likelihood estimator $\widehat{\theta}$ is very sensitive to small changes in the data. One might imagine that updating would be done periodically, leading to occasional substantial jumps in the estimator. Is this reasonable? For n=100, the MLE ranges from 0.00-0.05 as the number of defaults ranges from 0 to 5 (the last value is incredibly unlikely). The posterior mean ranges in the same case from 0.0036 to 0.011, and the posterior mode lies on a similar range slightly left shifted. Which are more reasonable estimates of the true underlying default probabilities? Further, note that the usual estimator for the standard deviation of the maximum-likelihood estimator gives 0 when no defaults are observed. This is surely unacceptable. The major differences between the posterior statistics ($\overline{\theta}$ and $\dot{\theta}$) and $\widehat{\theta}$ occur at extremely unusual samples, for example the five-default sample in the 100-observation case. But what would be the modeler's reaction to such a sample? Would it be that the default probability for this portfolio, thought to be an extremely safe portfolio, is indeed 0.05? Or, would the reaction be that there is something unusual happening, signaling a need for further investigation. Perhaps it is just a very unusual sample (in which case the estimate $\widehat{\theta}$ is very unusual and it might be better to stick with $\overline{\theta}$ as an indication of the actual default probability). Or perhaps some assets have been misclassified or there are other errors in the data. Or, perhaps, economic conditions have become so dire that a portfolio with a 5% default is a low-default portfolio. If so, surely some other hints that things are not going well would be available.

8 Information

In many applications, including the present application to default probabilities, the approaches via posterior distribution statistics and maximum likelihood agree for "large" samples. The logic of the argument is that the likelihood function depends on the sample size n, and thus information in the sample is increasing with n. On the other hand, the information in the prior is fixed and not increasing with the sample size. Thus, for large enough samples, the prior can be ignored, since the inference based on the posterior distribution will approach the inference based on the likelihood as the likelihood information dominates the prior information. Formally, the information in the likelihood is $O(n)$, while the prior information is $O(1)$. Now, information is not easily measured, but one widely accepted local measure of information is the curvature of the logarithm of the likelihood or prior around the maximum. This is measured by the negative second derivative, as 2.3 for the likelihood function and $(\alpha - 1)/(t - a)^2 + (\beta - 1)/(b - t)^2$ for the prior. Evaluated at the MLE $\widehat{\theta}$ with in addition the expectation taken over r with respect to the prior $p(\theta|e)$, these numbers are 42206, 126619, and 211032 for n= 100, 300 and 500. Note that this is not the Fisher Information, since the expectation is taken with respect to the prior, rather than for the true but unknown distribution or more commonly, relying on the continuous mapping theorem, for the distribution corresponding to $\widehat{\theta}$ (which is r/n, and therefore disturbingly self referential). The negative second derivative of the log of prior distribution evaluated at the prior mode is 203689. Thus the prior information is quantitatively substantially more important than the sample information for the n=100 and 300 cases, and just as important at the large sample value of 500. This is an unlikely sample size for our conjectural portfolio of loans to highly rated large banks. It would take vastly more data before the likelihood dominated the prior. There are a number of other measures of the information in a random variable or the relative information between a pair of random variables (or distributions). These lead to different numerical particulars but the same message: the importance of the prior information in any practical analysis simply cannot be ignored.

9 Continuing Issues

The approach suggested here raises a number of issuers worthy of further treatment or comment.

9.1 Assessment and combination of expert information

There is a large literature on probability assessment. Much of this focusses on experts who are not necessarily familiar with formal probability concepts. The situation is somewhat simpler here, as the experts are used to dealing with probabilities and thinking about the ways probabilities combine (but not necessarily with assessing uncertainty about parameters in probabilistic terms). Thinking about small probabilities is notoriously difficult; Kahneman and Tversky (1974) began a large literature. What are the easiest probability questions to assess when constructing a prior distribution? What are the most informative questions, in terms of tying down prior parameters tightly? How should information be fed back to the expert for revision? How should information from several experts be combined? This is addressed by Garthwaite, Kadane, and O'Hagan (2005), Lindley, Tversky, and Brown (1979) and many others. Here there are essentially two reasonable possibilities. Answers to the same question from different experts can simply be entered into the GMM calculation as separate equations. Alternatively, they could be averaged as repeated measurements on the same equation (the difference here is only one of weighting). Or, the prior specification could be done for each expert m, and the results combined in a mixture, $p(\theta|e_1,...,e_m) = \sum_m \alpha_m p(\theta|e_m)$, where α_m is the nonnegative weight assigned to the mth expert and $\sum_m \alpha_m = 1$. This procedure should be combined with feedback to the experts and subsequent revision.

9.2 Robustness

The issue of robustness of the inference about the default probability arises at the validation stage. Modelers can expect to have to review their prior assessment mechanisms with validators and to provide justification for the methods used. This is no different from the requirements for any other method of estimation of the default probability (and other required parameters). Prudent modelers will report not only the posterior distribution of θ as well as its mean $\bar{\theta}$ but summary statistics and any interesting or unusual features of the dataset. "Surprises" in the data will have to be explained. This is not specific to the Bayesian approach, but applicable to any method used. Bayesian robustness issues, and procedures for assessing robustness of results, are described by Berger and Berliner (1986). Some experimentation shows that inferences are not particularly sensitive to specification of the parameters a and b, as long as r/n is in the interval $[a, b]$, as expected. Thus, primary attention should be paid to the determination of α and β. Robustness is closely related to issues of supervision, as supervisors will review both the modeling efforts and the validation procedures of institutions.

9.3 Relation to Bernoulli Mixture Models

Giesecke and Weber (2004) provide a model leading to a mixture model for defaults quite similar in mathematical form to our model. The models are conceptually quite different, as the prior distribution for θ in our model reflects the state of information about the default probabilities, while in mixture models the distribution represents a physical mechanism. In Giesecke and Weber (2004) that mechanism includes a random element in θ, generated by interactions in the economy, as well as systematic variation generated by a regressor – a "risk driver" in Baselspeak (see Basel Committee on Banking Supervision (2005)). Adding risk drivers to our formulation is a matter for future development. Here we focus on conceptual issues in the simplest and most widely specified model.

9.4 Supervision

Subjectivity enters every statistical analysis. For many problems, data information is substantial and the subjective elements are perhaps less important. In the present setting subjectivity enters explicitly in the specification of $p(\theta|r,e)$. Subjectivity also enters in specification of $p(D|\theta,e)$, but we are used to that and the explicit dependence on judgement is usually dropped. Similarly, subjectivity enters in the classification of assets into "homogeneous" groups and many other places in settings involving supervision. Supervisors generally insist that the decisions made at the modeling level be logically based and validated. Thus, supervisors are willing to accept subjective decisions, as long as they are well grounded. It is a small additional step to add subjective information about plausible parameter values. There should be evidence that due consideration was given to specification of $p(\theta|r,e)$ (as well as the current requirement that $p(D|\theta,e)$ be justified). As in the case of validation, examples can be provided and standards set, while still relying on banks to perform their own analyses and validation. Newsletter No. 6 was written by the Basel Committee Accord Implementation Group's Validation Subgroup in response to banking industry questions and concerns regarding portfolios with limited loss data. Problem portfolios are those for which a "calculation based on historic losses ... would not be sufficiently reliable to form the basis of a probability of default estimate...."(p.1) The newsletter notes that problem portfolios are also those which "may not have incurred recent losses, but historical experience or other analysis might suggest that there is a greater likelihood of losses than is captured in recent data."(p.1). The implication is that the actual probability of default is greater than the measured default rate. This case clearly points to disagreement between data information and a prior, where the prior is explicitly based on other data ("historical experience," not in the current sample) or expert opinion ("other analysis"). The newsletter does not suggest impossible mechanical solutions and instead sticks to sensible recommendations like getting more data. A section heading in the newsletter reads as follows: "A relative lack of loss data can at times be compensated for by other methods for assessing risk parameters." This is precisely what I am proposing. In reference to the Basel II document itself (Basel Committee on Banking Supervision (2004)), the newsletter quotes paragraph 449: "Estimates must be based on historical experience and empirical evidence, and not based purely on subjective or judgmental considerations." This seems to allow both data and nondata information, but not exclusively the latter, and thus to hold open the possibility of combining data evidence with nondata evidence in the formal system of conditional probability. Paragraph 448 notes that "estimates of PD, LGD and EAD must incorporate all relevant, material and available data, information, and methods." This seems to make a distinction between data and other sources of information, which is consistent with our analysis.

One danger is that an institution could claim about a bizarre assessment that it is the prior assessment of an expert who predicts no defaults. And indeed, it might be true. There are a lot of experts. Thus some standards will be necessary, not just showing that the prior uncertainly was rigorously assessed, but that it meets some general standards of reliability. If asset groups were standardized across banks, then an agency could provide standardized descriptions of expert opinion. Supervisors do not currently seem to think such standardization appropriate or desirable. Could the agencies nevertheless provide some guidance? I think this would be feasible. Newsletter 6 states (p.4), "Supervisors expect to continue to share their experience in implementing the Framework in the case of LDPs in order to promote consistency." Could this mean that supervisors will share expert information to be incorporated into each bank's analysis? Clearly, the role of the supervisor, used to dealing with less formal subjectivity, will have to be defined when it comes to formal (probabilistically described) subjective information.

10   Conclusion

I have considered inference about the default probability for a low-default portfolio on the basis of data information and expert judgement. Examples consider sample sizes of 100, 300, and 500 for hypothetical portfolios of loans to very safe, highly-rated large banks. The sample sizes of 100 and 300 are perhaps most realistic in this setting. I have also represented the judgement of an expert in the form of a probability distribution, for combination with the likelihood function. This prior distribution seems to reflect expert opinion fairly well. Errors, which would be corrected through feedback and respecification in practice, are likely to introduce more certainty into the distribution rather than less. There are no real data here; the portfolios are hypothetical. Nevertheless, it is possible to study the posterior distributions for all of the most likely configurations of defaults in the samples. In each case, the modal number of defaults is small. In the sample of 500, two defaults are expected. I have reported results for zero defaults through a number of defaults above any reasonable likelihood. In all of these, the sample information contributes rather little relative to the expert information. Although real data are not included, bounds for the likely value for the default probability (the most likely value and the expected value) are fairly tight within the relevant range of data possibilities. Thus, the data variability which is reasonably expected, and indeed data variability which is highly unlikely, will not affect sensible inference about the default probability beyond the second decimal place. These results raise issues about how banks should treat estimated default probabilities and how supervisors should evaluate both procedures and outcomes for particular portfolios.

References

BALTHAZAR, L. (2004): "PD Estimates for Basel II," *Risk*, April, 84–85.

BASEL COMMITTEE ON BANKING SUPERVISION (2004): "International Convergence of Capital Measurement and Capital Standards: A Revised Framework," Bank for International Settlements.

——— (2005): "Basel Committee Newsletter No. 6: Validation of Low-Default Portfolios in the Basel II Framework," Discussion paper, Bank for International Settlements.

BERGER, J., AND L. M. BERLINER (1986): "Robust Bayes and Empirical Bayes Analysis with Contaminated Priors," *The Annals of Statistics*, 14(2), 461–486.

BERGER, J. O. (1980): *Statistical Decision Theory: Foundations, Concepts and Methods*. Springer-Verlag.

BOX, G. E. P., AND G. C. TIAO (1992): *Bayesian Inference in Statistical Analysis*. New York: John Wiley & Sons.

CHALONER, K. M., AND G. T. DUNCAN (1983): "Assessment of a Beta Prior Distribution: PM Elicitation," *The Statistician*, 32(1/2, Proceedings of the 1982 I.O.S. Annual Conference on Practical Bayesian Statistics), 174–180.

DeGroot, M. H. (1970): *Optimal Statistical Decisions*. McGraw-Hill.

Diaconis, P., and D. Ylvisaker (1985): "Quantifying Prior Opinion," in *Bayesian Statistics 2*, ed. by J. M. Bernardo, M. H. DeGroot, D. Lindley, and A. Smith, pp. 133–156. Elsevier Science Publishers BV (North-Holland).

Garthwaite, P. H., J. B. Kadane, and A. O'Hagan (2005): "Statistical Methods for Eliciting Probability Distributions," *Journal of the American Statistical Association*, 100, 780–700.

Giesecke, K., and S. Weber (2004): "Cyclical Correlations, Credit Contagion and Portfolio Losses," *Journal of Banking and Finance*, 28, 3009–3036.

Jaynes, E. T. (2003): *Probability Theory: The Logic of Science*. New York: Cambridge University Press.

Kadane, J. B., J. M. Dickey, R. L. Winkler, W. S. Smith, and S. C. Peters (1980): "Interactive Elicitation of Opinion for a Normal Linear Model," *Journal of the American Statistical Association*, 75(372), 845–854.

Kadane, J. B., and L. J. Wolfson (1998): "Experiences in Elicitation," *The Statistician*, 47(1), 3–19.

Kahneman, D., and A. Tversky (1974): "Judgement Under Uncertainty: Heuristics and Biases," *Science*, 185, 1124–1131.

Lindley, D. V. (1953): "Statistical Inference," *Journal of the Royal Statistical Society. Series B (Methodological)*, 15(1), 30–76.

———— (1982): "The Improvement of Probability Judgements," *Journal of the Royal Statistical Society. Series A (General)*, 145(1), 117–126.

Lindley, D. V., A. Tversky, and R. V. Brown (1979): "On the Reconciliation of Probability Assessments," *Journal of the Royal Statistical Society. Series A (General)*, 142(2), 146–180.

OCC (2006): "Validation of Credit Rating and Scoring Models: A Workshop for Managers and Practitioners," in *Validation of Credit Rating and Scoring Models*.

Pluto, K., and D. Tasche (2005): "Thinking Positively," *Risk*, August, 72–78.

RAIFFA, H., AND R. SCHLAIFER (1961): *Applied Statistical Decision Theory.* Harvard Business School.

ZELLNER, A. (1996): *Introduction to Bayesian Inference in Econometrics.* New York: John Wiley & Sons.